BROKEN BY ACCIDENT

Finding Purpose in Your Stories

Gwen Ebner

Path to Wholeness Publishing

Broken by Accident: Finding Purpose in your Stories
© 2020 by Pathway to Wholeness Publishing

Printed in the United States of America
ISBN 978-0-9981787-2-1

Each Spiritual Formation Experience used by permission from Dr. Thom
Gardner.

Scripture quotations marked NIV are taken from the Holy Bible, New
International Version copyright © 1973, 1978, 1984, 2011 by Biblica, Inc. Used by
permission of Zondervan Publishing. All rights reserved worldwide.

Scripture quotations marked NLT are taken from the New Living Translation,
copyright © 1996, 2004. Used by permission of Tyndale House. All rights
reserved.

Scriptural quotations marked MSG are taken from THE MESSAGE, copyright ©
2003 by Eugene Peterson. Used by permission of NavPress Publishing Group.
All rights reserved.

Scripture quotations marked TPT are from The Passion Translation. Copyright
© 2017, 2018 by Passion & Fire Ministries, Inc. Used by permission. All rights
reserved.

Scripture quotations marked ERV are taken from the "HOLY BIBLE: EASY-TO-
READ VERSION" © 2001 by World Bible Translation Center, Inc. and used by
permission.

Scripture quotations marked ISV are taken from the Holy Bible: International
Standard Version. Copyright © 1996-forever by The ISV Foundation. ALL
RIGHTS RESERVED INTERNATIONALLY. Used by permission.

Scriptures marked THE VOICE are taken from the THE VOICE (The Voice):
Scripture taken from THE VOICE ™. Copyright© 2008 by Ecclesia Bible Society.
Used by permission. All rights reserved and used by permission.

Contents

How to Use this Book

Maybe you're like me and have failed to see the value of the pain that took place in your childhood. This discovery led me to begin writing out my stories.

I was encouraged by my Writer's Group to not just say how I felt (i.e., I'm afraid), but to show what my feelings felt like (my heart was pounding). As I did this, it began to trigger emotions stored deep inside me. I went to see a counselor and she assisted me in processing my feelings and mourning my losses.

This helped me see that a lot of good had come from my stories. So, I decided to write a second version, reframing the meaning of each story and how it had helped me grow. It became even more exciting when I contacted family members and found inspiring additions to these stories.

I was so excited about this process that I decided to show my readers how to do this for themselves. To help you, I have offered the following format in each chapter:

- One of my childhood stories, followed by how I found purpose in that story
- A chance for you to journal about one of your stories

- A Scriptural meditation that will assist you in having a time with God, allowing you to reinforce God's truth
- A chance for you to find purpose in your story
- Some moments of reflection as you complete a coloring page

You can go through this book as an individual or as a group. In Appendix E, you will find some ideas for leading a group through this study.

If you find yourself emotionally triggered by your own stories, consider seeing a counselor or a pastor. Appendix F has some suggestions for resources and counselors.

I have provided you with the opportunity to go deeper in your healing process. See the additional information in Appendix D on how to do this.

I have also included additional ideas to help you as you go through this book. These ideas will show up in a box within the chapter. May you find freedom and hope as you find purpose in your stories.

Continue to work out your salvation … for it is God who works in you to will and to act in order to fulfill his good purpose. (Phil. 2:12-13, NIV)

Introduction

As I sat on the deck of a chalet in Buena Vista, Colorado, I found myself staring at the massive fourteeners in front of me. The beauty and majesty of these mountains were enough to take my breath away. Only God could have fashioned such splendor and possessed the ability to create such magnificence.

Regrettably, I had spent my life spinning a lot of plates because I felt worthless and unlovable. But while sitting on this deck, a thought bubbled up in me: God wanted me to be free, so his creativity could flow through me. I would be like those mountains in front of me: majestic because he designed me; sturdy because his power was in me; and fearfully and wonderfully made, because I bore his image.

As I gazed at the splendor before my eyes, I found God giving me the outline and title for a new book, Broken by Accident. I hadn't planned to write a book. I had only promised to cook for this retreat, but God had something else in mind. He wanted to use my stories.

For years I had stuffed my past inside me, and all I could feel was hurt. This hurt not only blocked my creativity but also my relationship with God. However, one day I stumbled on this advice in the book of Isaiah, "Forget about what's happened; don't keep going over old history. Be alert, be present. (For) I'm about to do something brand-new. It's bursting out! Don't you see it? (Isa. 43:18-19, Message) Yes, I did see it! God wanted to use my stories to not only heal me but also to help others. So, I eagerly began writing them out.

The first story that came to mind began in the fall of 1949, the year my father decided to buy a laundry business. He felt that this would be a way to support Mom and my sister, one-year-old Donna. Since Dad wasn't able to pay any employees, he and Mom would have to work 12-15 hours a day.

But a shockwave hit my mom that November when she discovered she was pregnant with a second child - me! She felt frustrated and overwhelmed and told Dad that she could not handle another baby right now; she could hardly take care of one-year-old Donna and work all day. She began speaking her frustrations out loud, "How could this have happened to me? I don't want another baby right now." I believe it was possible that mom's words and stress was being transmitted to me, an infant in her womb.

Mom continued working as I grew in her womb. On Saturday, July 15th, Mom worked an exhausting day and finally climbed into bed. However, at early dawn, she roused with twitches in her stomach. It didn't take long for her to realize she needed to head to the hospital. When they arrived, her contractions were so close together that they took her right up to the maternity ward, while Dad checked her in. By the time Dad made it upstairs, Gwendolyn Dolores had already arrived. Mom would later say that she almost delivered me in the hospital elevator.

After three days in the hospital, Dad came to take us home. Within a week, Mom was working again. In order to get her work done, Mom had to leave me lying in a playpen most of the day. She began bragging to other people, "Gwen is such a good baby; she hardly ever cries."

Finding Purpose in the Story: Reframing its Meaning

A couple weeks after my birth, Grandma Katy, Mom's mother, called and asked how she and I were doing. Mom told Grandma Katy that she had to leave me in a playpen most of the time to get her work done. The irritation was obvious in Grandma's voice as she said, "I will be coming there tomorrow to take care of Gwenie. She is not going to be left in a playpen all day!" My Grandma Katy stayed for four weeks, caring for me with a mother's love. I can only surmise that the personal touch and attention she gave me as a newborn had a positive effect on me. Even today, it's hard for me to believe that a woman with nineteen children, fifty-eight grandchildren, and a number of great grandchildren would take time to offer me this kind of sacrificial love.

Throughout my adult years, we moved a lot with my husband's career. But I was blessed to live near my mom and dad numerous times. And then as they began to age, they decided to move to Findlay, Ohio where I lived. During that time, Mom and I were able to share many memories and support each other during Dad's strokes and his death in 2012. What a blessing that was for me to have that connection with them.

I finally realized that Mom's statement, "I don't want another baby right now" was not really about me, but about bad timing. One day I stumbled upon these words, "I have made you a part of me, written you on the palms of my hands" (Isa. 49:16, Voice). It was amazing that God had always wanted me, even before I was born. I was valuable enough that he would write my name on the palms of his hands!

This scripture also assured me that God loved and valued me:

You (God) know me inside and out, you know every bone in my body; You know exactly how I was made, bit by bit, how I was sculpted from nothing into something. Like an open book, you watched me grow from conception to birth; all the stages of my life were spread out before you, The days of my life all prepared before I'd even lived one day.

Psalm 139:14-16 (MSG)

CHAPTER 1

❦

*B*roken by *A*ccident

My 5-year-old eyes danced as I matched Mom's quick steps and leaped into our 1952 green and white Nash. On this bright and sunny day, we were headed to the store to buy curtains for the house we had just moved into. But we had to hurry because the store closed at 6 pm on Saturday and didn't open again until Monday morning.

Once we were on our way, I began curiously looking out the window from one side to the other. This road wasn't the one we normally took to town. We were taking a shortcut which was sparsely populated with farmhouses and had a river running parallel to it.

I was surprised at how fast mom was driving around the curve ahead of us. Before I knew it, our car was spinning in the gravel, and headed into the woods. All of a sudden, I felt a jolt as we crashed into a tree. We had barely missed that scary river in front of our eyes!

Mom's head was thrown into the windshield and her right leg was pinned between the seat and the dashboard. I got thrown from the car, and my left elbow was cut. My head began to pound, but I was distracted by the blood I was seeing coming from Mom's ankle. I cried out, "Mommy, it looks like you are hurt. Are you okay?" She assured me she was all right, but I doubted it because I saw the blood flowing from her ankle. She began to push and pull as she tried to free herself.

Mom finally gave up because it was obvious, she was pinned in the car. She happened to see a man off the side of the road, changing a flat tire. She decided to lay on the horn to get his attention. I'll never forget its shrieking sound, but thankfully he heard it and began to walk quickly toward our car. His face looked tense as he eyed our smashed car, and my mother trapped in it. He and Mom recognized each other because he was a friend of one of her brothers. He agreed to rush to a nearby farmhouse and call for help.

By now, I could barely breathe. Was my mom going to die if this bleeding didn't stop? My fear seemed to grow bigger and bigger. It was hard to look at Mom because of all the blood that kept flowing from her leg. I finally breathed a sigh of relief when I heard the sound of help arriving. The men used a blowtorch to get mom out of the car.

The men put mom into the ambulance and allowed me to sit beside her. I held her hand as we traveled to the hospital. In a quivering voice, I said, "Mommy, are you going to be okay?" She kept assuring me that she was okay.

When we arrived at the hospital, they took us to the ER. I kept my eyes focused on Mom. Sometimes she was awake; at other times, she seemed to be asleep. I heard the doctor say they could hardly detect Mom's pulse and that she was in shock. But what frightened me the most was that her leg continued to drip blood, and her ankle began to turn black. I had never seen Mom hurt like this. The doctor even mentioned amputating her leg.

My dad arrived at the hospital as soon as he found out about the accident. I could tell he was upset because he was demanding that the doctors continue working to save Mom's leg.

Dad telephoned Grandma Katy from the hospital's payphone to let her know about our accident. She did the only thing she knew to do; she began calling nearby churches and asking for prayer. A short time later, the doctor returned to Mom's bedside and, with a look of astonishment said, "Something has happened! Her foot is no longer bleeding. I think we can save it." They were able to reattach Mom's foot to her leg with steel pins. They also connected her broken hip with a steel pin.

The nurse told me that I would be staying the night because I had suffered a blow to my head and had a concussion. My heart pounded at the thought of leaving my mom and being in the hospital all alone. As I settled into my room, they offered me my supper. But my stomach was queasy, and it was difficult for me to eat the food they brought. I even turned down ice cream, my favorite dessert.

I was released from the hospital on Sunday. I was quiet and withdrawn as Dad drove me back to our house. But when I got home, I began begging him to let me skip school on Monday. He finally agreed that I could, but insisted I return on Tuesday.

Just thinking about leaving the house made me feel nervous and jittery, so I asked my seven-year-old sister if she would meet me at noon when my bus arrived and walk me to my kindergarten class. Relief came over me as she securely held my hand and walked me there.

A week later, I frantically ran out of the house when I began to smell smoke. A nearby neighbor called for help, and the firemen were able to save our home, even though we had a lot of smoke damage.

After the accident, I had trouble feeling safe. Often, I resisted leaving the house; but now even our house wasn't safe anymore. Our car had been demolished in the accident, so every time I got in the new vehicle Dad had bought, I trembled. Even going to sleep at night was hard. My mind would repeatedly recall the blood I had seen coming from Mom's leg.

My mother spent a month in the hospital, and that was the longest month of my life! Finally, on Mother's Day, my dad said we would be allowed to see Mom. As I walked into her hospital room, I saw a smile show up on her face. Mom was going to be all right.

A week later, my heart leaped with joy when Dad brought Mom home. I became her little helper, watching over her. But my bubble burst within a week when Mom fell while walking with her crutches at a family reunion. I couldn't believe it. Sadness filled my heart as I realized that she was going back to the hospital, where she ended up staying for two more weeks.

No one ever talked to me about what happened during this traumatic event. So, I had no opportunity to process my feelings during childhood. I ended up losing my childlike joy and my world no longer felt safe.

~ From this experience, I had _feelings_ of insecurity, and I didn't feel safe.

~ The _lie_ I believed was that I wasn't safe at home, school, in our car, or away from my mom.

~ The way I _coped_ with these feelings was to order my life and environment. I also used control to help me feel in charge of my life.

Finding Purpose in My Story: Reframing its Meaning

I could hardly sit still because Mom and I were finally going to have "mommy and me" time. I rarely had time with Mom because a baby sister had been added to our family just five months earlier. And I was excited to go with Mom and help her buy some curtains for the house we had just bought.

I could tell that Mom was in a hurry that day. Our stores closed on Saturday afternoon and didn't open again until Monday. As we traveled toward town, I realized Mom was taking a different route than she usually took. And before I knew it, we had spun into the woods. But we were so lucky to have hit that tree instead of heading into the foreboding river. It was obvious we had received a miracle when six months later, another family spun into the same woods and plunged into the river. The father and mother, plus their three children, drowned that day.

Mom had severely wounded her leg because of the impact of the tree that had penned her in. She had also lost a lot of blood, but when she saw a man in the distance, changing a flat tire, she laid on the horn until he noticed her. Her action that day, served as a call for help. The man turned out to be a friend of mom's brother and recognized her.

When my Grandma Katy learned how serious Mom's injuries were, she felt led to call eight churches in the area and ask for prayer. I believe "the prayer of a righteous person is powerful and effective" (James 5:16), and these prayers helped save my mom's leg. Grandma Katy had also taken care of me as a newborn when mom was busy in the laundry. She selflessly came to our rescue again and tended to the needs of my sisters and me for six weeks as Mom healed.

We were astonished by the support we received from our neighbors. They brought food to us, and many in the neighborhood went to the hospital and gave blood that helped save Mom's life.

Mom ended up with some severe injuries, an ankle that was severed from her leg, hanging on only by a piece of skin, and a broken hip. She had to go through many complicated skin grafts and other surgeries. However, just the right doctor with the expertise she needed was available that evening. Despite her serious injuries, Mom ended up living a long life to the ripe old age of 90.

I was thrown out of the car but landed into some brush, rather than another tree. These bushes kept me from hitting a nearby tree, which was a miracle of God.

My mom was traumatized by this accident and vowed that she would never drive a car again. But through the loving encouragement and insistence of my dad, Mom slowly got back into the car and began to drive again. What a blessing for our family that Mom was able to drive us to places we needed to go throughout our childhood.

BEFORE YOU START WRITING OUT YOUR FIRST STORY,
CONSIDER TAKING THE 'FEELING PROFILE 1'
IN APPENDIX A TO FIND OUT WHICH FEELING IS YOUR
STRONGEST ONE AND WHAT IT LOOKS LIKE WHEN YOU
MOVE TO MORE POSITIVE FEELINGS.

Your Story

Recall a story (preferably in your childhood) when you felt insecure or unsafe. In the lines below, write where you were, your age and the situation that took place.

_____

_____

_____

_____

_____

_____

_____

_____

_____

_____

Connecting with God

We will use a scriptural process to experience the heart of God, which can help us work through our feelings about our story.

Choose a scripture (below) that reinforces God's Truth about feeling secure and safe. I have provided a spiritual formation experience after these scriptures that you can follow.

The eternal God is your refuge, and his everlasting arms are under you. (Deut. 33:27, NLT)

God is a safe place to hide, ready to help when we need him. (Psa. 46:1, MSG)

The name of the LORD is a strong fortress; the godly run to him and are safe. (Prov. 18:10, NLT)

Just as the mountains surround Jerusalem, so the Lord's wrap-around presence surrounds his people, protecting them now and forever. (Psa. 125:2, TPT)

Because you are my helper, I sing for joy in the shadow of your wings. I cling to you; your strong right hand holds me securely. (Psa. 63:7-8, NLT)

Spiritual Formation Experience

Recall a place from your personal history that felt safe.
Imagine God being there with you.

Meditate on the verse of scripture that you chose above,
saying it softly, over & over to yourself until you can
say it or a portion of it with your eyes closed. (As you
repeat this scripture, allow yourself to see it with the
eyes of your heart.)

Journal your response to these questions:

1. What is the picture you see in your mind's eye as you
repeat the scripture?

_____

_____

_____

_____

2. What does the scripture reveal about the heart of
God?

_____

_____

_____

_____

3. Put yourself in the picture of this scripture. What is the Lord speaking to you personally in this scripture?

_____

_____

_____

_____

4. Take time to pray, saying to God what you have seen and heard from Him today through this experience.

Finding Purpose in Your Story: Reframing its Meaning

Think back on the story you wrote about feeling insecure or unsafe. Here are some questions to help you in finding a purpose for your story:

What has God taught you, and how have you grown as a result of this story?

_____

_____

_____

_____

What are some good things that have come from it (blessings, coincidences, miracles, healing, etc.)?

_____

_____

_____

_____

Color and Share

Studies show that coloring can help you slow down your heart rate, giving you a sense of calm. Try concentrating only on coloring in a non-competitive way, and you will experience a change in your feelings and mood. To print additional journal or coloring pages, go to GwenEbner.com/free.

While you color on the page I have provided, share with God (in prayer) or with someone else how you have found purpose in your story. *(Feel free to use your answers from the questions above.)*

If you are sharing your thoughts with God, you can do it out loud or write it on the lines below:

_____

_____

_____

_____

_____

_____

_____

_____

Check out the extra information in Appendix D if you want to go deeper in this healing process.

JESUS

You are my
Hiding Place

CHAPTER 2

❧

Wanting Love and Attention

My mind could not settle down after the car accident. It didn't help that two weeks after Mom returned home, she fell using her crutches and had to return to the hospital. My brain kept telling me something terrible was going to happen to my mom. So, I continually watched her for fear that she would have another mishap.

One of our family rituals was to ride a New York Central train to Florida every spring to see Grandpa Glen and Grandma India. I remember the smell of orange blossoms filling the air as we got closer to their house. And the Florida sun felt amazing after our cold Ohio winter.

But this year was different because Grandpa Glen had died of a heart attack shortly after our terrible car accident. Dad ended up going alone to Grandpa Glen's funeral because Mom was still healing from her injuries. I felt mixed up because I wanted to take care of Mom while Dad was gone, but I also needed to go and see for myself that Grandpa Glen was dead. Oh, how I wished that Dad would have let me go with him.

The following spring, we rode the train again to Florida to my grandparent's house. My 6-year-old heart felt stirred up. Dad told me that Grandpa Glen had died, but I couldn't believe it.

As I entered my grandparent's house, I felt like my world had fallen apart. Grandpa Glen wasn't there to hug and kiss me. It had felt like a bad dream, but now, I knew it was real. He had left me for good! How could he have done this to me?

Throughout the years, I had noticed that my sister Donna was Grandma India's favorite. Therefore, it felt right when Grandpa Glen paid attention to me. And as time went by, he and I became close.

However, after his death, Grandma India made it clear that Donna was her favorite, and now that Grandpa Glen was gone, I was left out. Her words cut through me like a knife. In a sense, I had not just lost Grandpa; I had lost Grandma India too.

Other things had also changed since he had died. Grandma India had taken in two roomers to help pay her bills. I particularly remember one of them, a man named Eddy. Right away, I seemed to be his favorite, and that made my heart flutter. Once Eddy began to pay attention to me, it took my mind off of my grandpa's absence. Eddy would talk to me and give me a lot of attention. He would hold me close to his body and kiss me on the cheek. Then he would tickle me until I began to laugh.

However, there was one thing about Eddy that I will never forget. He had a strange smile on his face when he pulled me close to him. I just figured it was because I was special to him.

One afternoon as Eddy and I were alone in the house, something strange happened. As he took me on his lap, I saw that weird look on his face again. It was then that

Mom unexpectedly came into the room and firmly spoke my name. She demanded that I go with her into Grandma India's bedroom. She looked furious, which made me wonder what I had done to make her so mad?

I avoided Eddy's eyes as I moved from his lap and followed my mom into the bedroom. She firmly closed the door and looked directly into my eyes. With a sharp voice, she said some words I will never forget, "Don't you EVER sit on his lap again. Do you hear me?" I began to tremble as I felt her disapproval. It must have been terribly wrong for me to sit on Eddy's lap. But he seemed to be a nice man, and he really liked me. So, this had to be my fault.

After that upsetting conversation with mom, I never again felt comfortable around Eddy. I avoided going near him so he wouldn't try to hold me. I began to guard my heart so that I could avoid the anger and disapproval that I had seen on Mom's face.

Within a year, Eddy got married and left Grandma India's house. I only saw him two times throughout the years that followed. Grandma India said that Eddy had married and divorced three times. The last time I remember seeing Eddy, he was in his 60's and had just married a tiny eighteen-year-old girl from another country.

I always wondered what Mom saw in Eddy's behavior that seemed inappropriate to her. When I was an adult, I asked her about this incident with Eddy. She chose not to tell me, only saying that Eddy was a 'dirty old man.'

~ After this situation, I had <u>feelings</u> of shame
~ The <u>lie</u> I believed was that because I did wrong, I was not okay.
~ The ways I <u>coped</u> with my feelings of shame was to keep my heart closed in relationships, especially with men.

Finding Purpose in My Story: Reframing its Meaning

As I look back over the five years that I spent with Grandpa Glen, I feel deeply grateful for the time I had with him. I'll never forget the loving relationship we had. I remember how he enjoyed fixing us breakfast; eggs and bacon, as well as pancakes. I could smell his cooking as soon as my eyes opened in the morning. And I will never forget the smile on his face and the hug he gave me when I arrived at his house.

As I look back on the situation with Eddy, I now realize that he was able to see my vulnerability. He knew how to make little girls feel precious, so that he could satisfy his own needs. But by God's grace, my mother was in the right place at the right time. I believe Eddy's body had given Mom a visual signal that he was ready to take advantage of me sexually.

As an adult, I decided to go to counseling. I began to understand that Mom's chilling words had protected me from childhood sexual abuse. He had already been touching and caressing me but had intentions of doing more. If she had not seen and realized what Eddy was up to, I could have been a victim of repeated sexual abuse.

I have met numerous women who were sexually abused, and many of them have ended up taking on addictions to alcohol or drugs to avoid their pain. Their sexual boundaries were broken early in life, and they became promiscuous. That helped me see this situation in a completely different way. Mom's intervention had shielded and protected me from an outcome like this. My new understanding allowed me to forgive Mom for her angry outburst and to see this in a new way.

It is also possible that some of Mom's anger may have resulted from abuse she had experienced herself. At one point, I did ask her if anyone had ever abused her; she simply said that she didn't remember anything from her childhood days.

During my teenage years and early twenties, I did date quite a few guys. I was often pressured in the area of sexuality but resisted the advances because of my experience with Eddy. Several men I dated were narcissistic, and two were unfaithful to me. Also, a man I trusted wounded me deeply.

I am thankful for the healing that God has done in this area of my life. I have been able to embrace a new belief about sexuality, one based on how God sees it. (Check out the book in Appendix F called, *Sacred Sex*.)

Your Story

Recall a story (preferably in your childhood) when you felt shame. In the lines below, write where you were, your age and the situation that took place.

_____

_____

_____

_____

_____

_____

_____

_____

_____

_____

_____

_____

_____

_____

Connecting with God

We will use a scriptural process to experience the heart of God, which can heal your feelings and correct the lies you have believed.

Choose a scripture (below) that reinforces God's Truth about the issue of shame. Then use that scripture to do a spiritual formation experience explained below.

For in Christ lives all the fullness of God in a human body. So you also are complete through your union with Christ. (Col. 2:9-10, NLT)

And the God of all grace, who called you to his eternal glory in Christ…will himself restore you and make you strong, firm and steadfast. (I Peter 5:10, NIV)

For we are God's masterpiece. He has created us anew in Christ Jesus, so we can do the good things he planned for us long ago. (Eph. 2:10, NLT)

But I will restore you to health and heal your wounds, declares the LORD. (Jer. 30:17, NIV)

Because of the Lord's gracious love we are not consumed, since his compassions never end. They are new every morning – great is your faithfulness! (Lam. 3:22-23, ISV)

Spiritual Formation Experience

Recall a place from your personal history that felt safe. Imagine God being there with you.

Meditate on the verse of scripture (that you chose above), saying it softly over & over to yourself until you can say it (or a portion of it) with your eyes closed. As you repeat the scripture, allow yourself to see it with the eyes of your heart.

Journal your response to these questions:

1. What is the picture you see in your mind's eye as you repeat the scripture?

_____

_____

_____

_____

2. What does the scripture reveal about the heart of God?

_____

_____

_____

_____

3. Put yourself in the picture of this scripture. What is the Lord speaking to you personally in this scripture?

_____

_____

_____

_____

4. Take time to pray, saying to God what you have seen and heard from Him today through this experience.

Finding Purpose in Your Story: Reframing its Meaning

Think back on the story you wrote about feeling shame. Here are some questions to help you in finding a purpose for your story:

What has God taught you, and how have you grown as a result of this story?

_____

_____

_____

_____

What are some good things that have come from it (blessings, coincidences, miracles, healing, etc.)?

_____

_____

_____

_____

Color and Share

Studies show that coloring can help you slow down your heart rate, giving you a sense of calm. Try concentrating only on coloring in a non-competitive way, and you will experience a change in your feelings and mood. To print additional journal or coloring pages, go to GwenEbner.com/free.

While you color on the page I have provided, share with God (in prayer) or with someone else how you have found purpose in your story. *(Feel free to use your answers from the questions above.)*

If you are sharing your thoughts with God, you can do it out loud or write it on the lines below:

_____

_____

_____

_____

_____

_____

_____

_____

_____

Check out the extra information in Appendix D if you want to go deeper in this healing process.

I am Complete in Christ

CHAPTER 3

Left Alone

My father worked for the railroad for 27 years. He began as an operator who controlled the track switches. He would pull devices that allowed the trains to move from one track to another. Occasionally, my dad would let me visit him at work. I would get a flutter in my stomach when he put his hand over mine and allowed me to help move those heavy-duty levers. At first, I thought I was doing it all by myself; later, I realized how heavy they really were.

But there was one thing I didn't like about my dad's job; it was his schedule. He had to work Swing Shifts - two days 7-3, then two days 3-11, and finally two days 11-7. Sometimes this meant he would miss some of our family activities.

It was 1957, and I was seven years old. I was sad when I learned that Dad had to work 3-11 pm on Christmas Eve. But Mom said that she had worked it out for the rest of us to go to a Christmas party at my aunt and uncle's house in the country. Having only one family car, though, required that we take Dad to work.

I had a hard time sitting still as we drove Dad to work. I felt a sigh of relief when we finally headed to my aunt and uncle's house. When we got there, I was able to play with my cousins in the basement until it was time to eat. After enjoying special holiday foods, we exchanged gifts and then enjoyed playing with the gifts we had received.

Before I knew it, the evening was over. Mom told us to put on our coats so we could head home. It wasn't long before the four of us were settled in our car and on our way. I began getting goosebumps all over me, even though I had on my winter coat. Why was it so cold tonight? Brrrrr!

We had driven for about ten minutes when all of a sudden, our car came to an abrupt stop. At first, Mom didn't know what was wrong. But finally, she realized that we had run out of gas. As I looked out the window,

I noticed that it was dark, and we were still in the country. Where would we find a gas station or phone booth out here? Mom said that she was sure another car would come by before long.

I began to shiver and shake. What were we going to do? We waited for what seemed like a long time. But finally, we heard a car coming down the road. I held my breath, hoping the people in the car would be able to help us.

The car stopped, and a man got out and asked if we needed help. Mom told him we had run out of gas. He said he wanted to help us, but his car was already full of family members and Christmas presents. But then he looked in our car and saw my two sisters and me. He hesitated but finally said that he might be able to squeeze my mom into the back seat and take her real quick to get some gas. With concern on her face, Mom asked if my two-year-old sister, Robyn, could come with her and sit on her lap. The man agreed.

My heart began to race as I realized that my 9-year-old sister and I would be left alone in the car. Mom assured us that the station was close by and that she'd be back in a few minutes. She settled us into the back seat and lovingly wrapped a blanket around our cold bodies.

After she left, tears began to gather in my eyes. It was scary being here all alone. Time seemed to pass by slowly as we waited on Mom to return. "I sure wish Mom would get back," I said to my sister. And then I would listen carefully to see if a car was coming down the road. At some point, I began to say to myself, "I don't care if I get any presents for Christmas this year. I just want my mommy to come back and take me home."

I began to think about another time when I was in a car and felt scared. Mom and I were in an accident and she was pinned in by the steering wheel, and almost bled to death. I remember being so scared and not knowing what to do. Oh, I don't like feeling this way again! Had something happened to my mommy again? Why wasn't that stranger bringing her back? It had been so long since she had left. And she had promised us that it would only be a few minutes before she came back.

I tried to go to sleep, but my shoulders felt tight, and I couldn't stop shaking. My sister Donna huddled closer to me, trying desperately to help both of us stay warm. She tried to reassure me that Mom would be back soon.

It seemed like forever before I heard a car coming down the road. My heart leaped with hope. Could it be Mom coming back? A sense of relief came over me when I saw the man and my mom get out of the car. I could see in Mom's eyes that she was sorry for being gone so long. She opened the car door and reached in and patted both of us.

She explained that when they got to the nearby station, it had already closed. They tried several other gas stations and then realized that everything had already shut down for Christmas Eve. Finally, she decided to call the man who owned the gas station where we usually bought gas. Once they found a phone booth, she called his home, and he was there. He offered to meet her at the station and give her some gas.

After the man put the gas in our car, we started for home. I have no idea what I got for Christmas the next day; I didn't even care. I was just glad that my mom had come back to get me!

The fear I felt that night would become a lasting memory. It had triggered my 5-year-old feelings of "I am scared and not feeling safe." After that experience, the same trigger would go off in me over and over again. It would follow this pattern: I feel upset, I am afraid, and I am not safe. Then I would attempt to take charge of my life, my surroundings, and sometimes even other people.

~ *From this experience, I had* _feelings_ *of fear.*
~ *The* _lie_ *I believed was that I was alone in my fear and had to deal with it myself.*
~ *The way I* _coped_ *with these feelings was to try to be in control of myself and my fearful situations.*

Finding Purpose in My Story: Reframing its Meaning

In 1957, many families had only one car because there was only one breadwinner in the family. That was true for my family. Consequently, Mom didn't often drive the family car since Dad needed it to go to work. He always took care of car maintenance, so she probably hadn't thought of checking the gas gauge that evening. I felt blessed that she could even drive again. She had insisted, after the severe accident in 1955, that she would never drive again.

It was a blessing that a car had come along that country road late that night. Most people knew that gas stations closed early on Christmas Eve and stayed closed through Christmas day. Thankfully, this family had traveled from another state and were late arriving at their relative's house.

Their car was so full of packages, people, and food that there was no room left. The father was touched when he saw a woman alone with three children late at night. He had his family push closer together so Mom could ride with them. They felt all right about leaving a 7 and 9-year-old alone, since the service station was close. They weren't thinking about the early closing of all stations.

When the closest service station was closed, Mom asked the man if he could drive her on into town to another station. After going from station to station, they realized there was going to be nothing open. Mom remembered the man who owned the station where they usually bought gas. But she had to look for a payphone, find the owner's phone number, give him time to get to the station and fill a gas can before she could head back to the car. This search for gas had taken at least an hour.

Two little girls sitting in a cold car in the dark for an hour, seemed like a long time. But I am forever grateful that I had my nine-year-old sister Donna with me as I waited for Mom to return. She nestled up close to me as we shared the blanket. Her soft voice was reassuring and being able to hold her hand was comforting. And I dare say that both of us were asking God to help our mommy come back. Donna had come to my rescue again. She had also held my hand and walked me to my kindergarten class after the accident two years before.

This incident taught me a new way of looking at gift giving. As a seven-year-old, my gift that year was having Mom return to get me!

Your Story

Recall a story (preferably in your childhood) when you felt afraid. In the lines below, write where you were, your age and the situation that took place.

_____

_____

_____

_____

_____

_____

_____

_____

_____

_____

_____

_____

_____

_____

_____

_____

Connecting with God

We will use a scriptural process to experience the heart of God, which can help us work through our feelings about our story.

Choose a scripture (below) that reinforces God's Truth about the issue of fear. Then use that scripture to do a spiritual formation experience that is explained below.

So do not fear, for I am with you; do not be dismayed, for I am your God. (Isa. 41:10, NIV)

I sought the LORD, and he answered me; he delivered me from all my fears. (Psa. 34:4, NIV)

When I am afraid, I put my trust in You. (Psa. 56:3, NIV)

For I am the LORD your God who takes hold of your right hand and says to you, 'Do not fear; I will help you'. (Isa. 41:13, NIV)

Where God's love is, there is no fear, because God's perfect love takes away fear. (I Jn. 4:18, ERV)

Spiritual Formation Experience

Recall a place from your personal history that felt safe. Imagine God being there with you.

Meditate on the verse of scripture that you chose above, saying it softly over & over to yourself until you can say it or a portion of it with your eyes closed. (As you repeat this scripture, allow yourself to see it with the eyes of your heart.)

Journal your response to these questions:

1. What is the picture you see in your mind's eye as you repeat the scripture?

_____

_____

_____

_____

2. What does the scripture reveal about the heart of God?

_____

_____

_____

_____

3. Put yourself in the picture of this scripture. What is the Lord speaking to you personally in this scripture?

_____

_____

_____

_____

4. Take time to pray, saying to God what you have seen and heard from Him today through this experience.

Finding Purpose in Your Story: Reframing its Meaning

Think back on the story you wrote about feeling afraid. Here are some questions to help you in finding a purpose for your story:

What has God taught you, and how have you grown as a result of this story?

_____

_____

_____

_____

What are some good things that have come from it (blessings, coincidences, miracles, healing, etc.)?

_____

_____

_____

_____

Color and Share

Studies show that coloring can help you slow down your heart rate, giving you a sense of calm. Try concentrating only on coloring in a non-competitive way, and you will experience a change in your feelings and mood. To print additional journal or coloring pages, go to GwenEbner.com/free.

While you color on the page I have provided, share with God (in prayer) or with someone else how you have found purpose in your story. *(Feel free to use your answers from the questions above.)*

If you are sharing your thoughts with God, you can do it out loud or write it on the lines below:

_____

_____

_____

_____

_____

_____

_____

_____

> *Check out the extra information in Appendix D if you want to go deeper in this healing process.*

A Life Filled With FAITH

CHAPTER 4

❧

The Price of Addiction

It has always been fun to see how people respond when I tell them that my mother was the twelfth child in a family of nineteen. I also have wondered what it would be like to have eighteen brothers and sisters.

However, I had some bragging rights myself. These aunts and uncles had birthed fifty-eight children! That meant I had a lot of first cousins, and some of them were around my age. Oh, what fun it was when we got together!

Every summer in June, the Millers had a family reunion. My heart began to leap for joy as I thought of all the activities that would take place at Armco Park. The playground was one of my favorite things, especially the swings. I would giggle as I kicked forward and backward as high as I could. And I squealed as I went flying recklessly down the slide and twirled round and round on the merry-go-round.

At some point, my aunts would call us together for lunch. I couldn't wait to eat Grandma Katy's chicken and dumplings and her homemade bread. My uncle Frank would catch a couple of turtles and make some tasty fried turtle. My mom always brought coleslaw, baked beans, and fresh green beans from our garden. There was a lot of delicious food to eat! However, I always kept my eye on the dessert table, so that I could make sure I got a piece of Aunt Laura's yummy butterscotch pie. I would sigh when Mom said I couldn't have dessert until I had eaten all the food on my plate.

After dinner, the men would start playing horseshoes, and the women would sit and talk ninety miles an hour as they cleaned up the table. Sometimes I would go on a walk with my two cousins, Cleta and Debbie. We would swing our arms and giggle as we shared our secrets. However, sometimes we weren't allowed to go off on our own because our aunts needed our help in babysitting our younger cousins. But this made me feel special because I was like a 'little mommy.'

Later in the afternoon, the uncles would announce that it was time for the annual softball game. The boys were so competitive and always wanted to win. They didn't want us girls on their team, but they allowed us to play. Then after the game, we would again gather around the picnic table and eat big pieces of cold watermelon. I had a burst of joy as I watched to see who could spit their watermelon seeds the farthest.

But with all the fun, there was still one thing about the reunion that made my heart sad – Grandpa Al. He always looked old, unhappy, and sort of scary. Did he even like coming to these reunions?

I felt jittery when I was around Grandpa Al. He sometimes asked me to sit on his lap, and when I did, I would get this weird feeling in my stomach when he looked at me. Also, Grandpa Al had an unpleasant smell about him. It wasn't anything I had every smelled before.

After the reunion one year, I asked Mom about his funny smell. She said Grandpa Al drank a lot of cheap wine and people called him a wino. She also said that wine caused him to do mean things to her and her family. And that she had decided she would never drink and hurt her children like he had.

One summer, mom paid a visit to our family doctor. She asked him what she could do about the pain she still felt from the car accident. The doctor's advice was for her to sip a little bit of whiskey when she was in pain. So secretly, Mom purchased some whiskey and hid it under the kitchen sink. When she felt pain, she would take a sip. But she wasn't satisfied with just a little bit, so she began to take more and more.

One day as I was playing in the living room, I began to feel thirsty. I made my way to the kitchen at the other end of our house. As I walked into the kitchen, I gasped in disbelief as I saw Mom lifting a bottle of whiskey to her mouth.

All of a sudden, Mom sensed that someone was in the room. As she turned around and saw me, there was embarrassment and shame on her face. Mom realized that I had seen her drinking. So, she took the bottle of whiskey and poured it down the drain. Then hurriedly, she threw the bottle in the garbage can.

This incident took Mom back to the horrible things she had experienced with her cruel alcoholic father. It also reminded her of the vow she had made never to expose her children to this dreadful experience. That was the last day my mother ever drank.

One day, Mom sat down to talk to my two sisters and me. She told us that Grandpa Al had died. I didn't feel very close to him, but I did breathe in sharply as Mom told us what had happened to him. He was cooking on his gas stove and had caught the cuff of his wool sweater on fire. Because he was so feeble, he was unable to pull it off of his body. So, he just sat down in a rocking chair and burned to death. I don't remember going to a funeral or even a memorial service for my grandpa. It was also sad that after his death, hardly anyone talked about Grandpa Al at family gatherings.

When I was older, I asked Mom about Grandpa Al. She said he had been a drunk for as long as she could remember. I felt sad for her as Mom told me stories about how Grandpa had been abusive to her, to Grandma Katy, and to her brothers and sisters. When he came home drunk, he would call my mom 'snake eyes' which scared her. She would run and hide behind her mom for fear of what he would do to her. Unfortunately, his addiction to alcohol was modeled to his children and passed on to three of my uncles and an aunt.

~ *From this experience, I had <u>feelings</u> of anxiety and uneasiness around my grandpa.*
~ *The <u>lie</u> I believed was that I needed to be in control of situations that made me feel anxious and uneasy.*
~ *The way I <u>coped</u> was with anxious avoidance. I tried to avoid people and situations that made me feel anxious, because I tended to take on other people's anxiety.*

Finding Purpose in the Story: Reframing its Meaning

I have many delightful memories from my mom's family, including family gatherings, reunions, and moments when we helped each other. Grandma Katy was a godly woman. She did all she could to raise nineteen children since Grandpa Al's drinking provided few resources for her and her children.

As adults, at least six of my aunts attended church regularly and had committed their lives to Christ. I had the privilege of attending the same church with Grandma Katy and two of these wonderful aunts.

I was always curious about Grandpa Al's family because of his brokenness and addiction to alcohol. I found out that his father was an alcoholic. However, he had a godly mother who was a short redhead like me. But she died when Grandpa Al was in his teens. After she died, his father was left to take care of all the children. Unfortunately, he and most of his brothers were alcoholics, just like their dad.

In 1940 Grandma told Grandpa Al that he had to move out of the house. Eventually she filed for a divorce. Grandpa found places to live and in 1952, he was invited to move in with one of my uncles and his family. Unfortunately, Grandpa Al continued to drink and influenced this uncle to drink with him. This drinking began to create family issues, so Grandpa Al was asked to leave their house.

This uncle had never been interested in going to church and having a relationship with Christ. However, in 1999 my uncle found out he had cancer. Thankfully, one of his daughters lovingly told him how he could receive Christ into his heart, and he did. I feel thankful that he had peace with God before he died.

Grandpa Al moved in with my Aunt Ethel. She kept encouraging him to go to church with her. He didn't want to go at first but finally began to go with her. After attending for a while, Grandpa Al gave his heart to Christ and was baptized at the church. My aunt said he was a different person after that and later expressed regret for how he had lived his life. What a miracle! I was filled with gratefulness when I learned about his change in heart.

There were three uncles and one aunt who were alcoholics. All of them got cancer later in life. Thankfully, during the time of their illnesses, all four of them committed their lives to Christ as well. A family member influenced three of them, and one was moved by the words of a chaplain in a VA hospital. I am grateful to know that all of them are in heaven today.

Your Story

Recall a story (preferably in your childhood) when you felt anxious or uneasy in a situation. In the lines below, write where you were, your age and the situation that took place.

_____

_____

_____

_____

_____

_____

_____

_____

_____

_____

_____

_____

_____

_____

_____

Connecting with God

We will use a scriptural process to experience the heart of God, which can help us work through our feelings about our story.

Choose a scripture (below) that reinforces God's Truth about the issue of anxiety or uneasiness. Then use that scripture to do a spiritual formation experience explained below.

Do not be anxious about anything, but in every situation, by prayer and petition, with thanksgiving, present your requests to God. And the peace of God, which transcends all understanding, will guard your hearts and your minds in Christ Jesus. (Phil. 4:6-7, NIV)

Cast all your anxiety on him because he cares for you. (I Peter 5:7, NIV)

When my anxious inner thoughts become overwhelming, your comfort encourages me. (Psa. 94:19, ISV)

Say to those with anxious hearts, 'Be strong, do not be afraid! Here is your God – he will save you'. (Isa. 35:4, ISV)

Don't be afraid, because I'm with you; don't be anxious, because I am your God. I keep on strengthening you; I'm truly helping you. (Isa. 41:10, ISV)

Spiritual Formation Experience

Recall a place from your personal history that felt safe. Imagine God being there with you.

Meditate on the verse of scripture that you chose above, saying it softly, over & over to yourself until you can say it or a portion of it with your eyes closed. (As you repeat this scripture, allow yourself to see it with the eyes of your heart.)

Journal your response to these questions:

1. What is the picture you see in your mind's eye as you repeat the scripture?

_____

_____

_____

_____

2. What does the scripture reveal about the heart of God?

_____

_____

_____

_____

3. Put yourself in the picture of this scripture. What is the Lord speaking to you personally in this scripture?

_____

_____

_____

_____

4. Take time to pray, saying to God what you have seen and heard from Him today through this experience.

Finding Purpose in Your Story: Reframing its Meaning

Think back on the story you wrote about feeling anxious or uneasy. Here are some questions to help you in finding a purpose for your story:

What has God taught you, and how have you grown as a result of this story?

_____

_____

_____

_____

What are some good things that have come from it (blessings, coincidences, miracles, healing, etc.)?

_____

_____

_____

_____

Color and Share

Studies show that coloring can help you slow down your heart rate, giving you a sense of calm. Try concentrating only on coloring in a non-competitive way, and you will experience a change in your feelings and mood. To print additional journal or coloring pages, go to GwenEbner.com/free.

While you color on the page I have provided, share with God (in prayer) or with someone else how you have found purpose in your story. *(Feel free to use your answers from the questions above.)*

If you are sharing your thoughts with God, you can do it out loud or write it on the lines below:

_____

_____

_____

_____

_____

_____

_____

_____

Check out the extra information in Appendix D if you want to go deeper in this healing process.

You are

Enough

CHAPTER 5

~

Holding on to Anger

As a child, my family bought most of our necessities in the downtown shopping area. My favorite place to shop was the Central Store, which was three floors high. I could hardly wait to ride on the elevator to the place where they sold children's clothes.

Every March, I was allowed to buy a new can-can slip to wear under my full-skirted dress for Easter. These slips cost somewhere between $1.99-$3.99, which was a lot of money. My heart would beat faster as I picked out a can-can slip, a pair of white gloves, and a matching hat to wear with my dress. I was a little nervous that Mom would think these things cost too much.

But after we got home from shopping, she was often unsatisfied with the item we had bought and would tell us we needed to return it to the store.

I remember how I timidly approached the counter to ask the lady for an exchange or refund. As a child, I didn't know how to tell the clerk what I needed. So, I would stutter, and my face would turn red as I tried to explain it to her. I began to feel angry. Why didn't Mom take it back instead of making my sister Donna and I do it?

I cannot tell you the number of times Mom changed her mind about things that she had purchased at the Central Store or ordered by catalog from Penney's or Sears. I inwardly became angry because I knew I would have to return them myself. And I dreaded doing that!

After a while, I realized that Mom had a difficult time making decisions. She ended up second-guessing herself so many times. And Mom's way of dealing with it was to make me take care of it, which left me feeling angry with her.

Mom also tended to hold her feelings in. Then, when

you least expected it, she'd blow up. It might be when I twirled around in a living room chair, or I failed to get her some water when she was hot from mowing the grass. How did I know what was important to her since she didn't tell me?

An unexpected 'blow up' took place one sunny day in summer when I was ten. As we were playing, Mom came flying into the room and shouted for us to get ready to leave. Her anger was evident, so we hurried to do what she said. We marched out the front door and walked on the circle-around porch to where our car was. As I fell in step beside her, I felt like my heart stopped beating when she told me that she was leaving Dad. As we drove to my aunt's house, I was quiet as I pondered what she had said. What had made her want to leave Dad?

We spent the day playing with my cousins and having lunch with them. I kept thinking about Mom's words and wondered what would happen if my parents got divorced. When it started getting dark, she told us to get back into the car. I was surprised when we pulled into our driveway at home.

I never understood why she was angry at Dad and marched out of the house. But she had modeled to me how to be angry and not deal with it properly.

Mom also tried to control me throughout my growing up years. At one point in school, I started playing the E flat horn. The band director said I had real talent and wanted me to start playing the French horn. He even said that the school would loan me an instrument to use. But Mom's response was to say that

I had to quit band, but I never knew why. She was also opposed to me trying out for cheerleading and I received no reason why.

Mom rarely allowed me to stay overnight at a friend's house or go to slumber parties. I was also seldom allowed to swim at our local pool, Chautauqua, with my friends.

Mom was pretty careful about what clothing she allowed me to buy. She usually controlled the outfits I could wear, what I could buy, or what I could sew.

These lessons not only affected me as a child but as an adult. Sometimes I didn't feel comfortable making my own decisions. Sometimes I was simply angry about her controlling my life and had no idea that I was stockpiling angry feelings way down deep inside me. The things I learned from my mom ended up affecting my responses throughout life.

~ *From this experience, I had _feelings_ of anger*
~ *The _lie_ I believed was that I had to allow others to control me*
~ *The way I _coped_ was to deny my feelings, so I could please others and make them happy*

Finding Purpose in My Story:
Reframing its Meaning

One day as I reflected on having to take back a lot of the things Mom and I had bought, God reminded me of something. My older sister, Donna, was always with me when we went back to the store. We had done it together! And I felt God say to me, "Gwen, I was always with you too!" That helped relieve my frustration about this situation.

My parents stayed married all my life. I was blessed and thankful when they came to their sixtieth wedding anniversary. Even though they had moments of frustration in their marriage, I was forever grateful that they had never gotten a divorce.

I do have to admit that Mom was controlling. However, I never doubted her love for me. Throughout her childhood, I realized that she had had so many hurtful things happen to her that she decided to protect us from being hurt like she had. This was one of her ways to show her love.

My mother didn't like us being out of her sight for very long. If I went on a date; she always stayed up until I came home. Today, I realize it was her way of staying connected with me and reminding me to use good judgment when on a date.

It was well known that we would be allowed to use Mom's sewing machine when we turned twelve years old. I could hardly wait until that birthday came, and she would teach me how to sew. I loved making wool skirts, and I was glad when she helped me pick out pretty sweaters to go with them. Her sister Bessie, my aunt, had boxes of fabric at her house and would let me pick out some that I liked. I was able to sew several pretty dresses every fall for school.

Mom was a fantastic gardener and had a love for flowers. I learned as a child to eat all kinds of fruits and vegetables and ended up with a love for gardening myself. We always ate a healthy diet, for which I will be forever grateful.

Your Story

Recall a story (preferably in your childhood) when you felt angry or allowed someone to control you. In the lines below, write where you were, your age and the situation that took place.

_____

_____

_____

_____

_____

_____

_____

_____

_____

_____

_____

_____

_____

_____

_____

_____

Connecting with God

We will use a scriptural process to experience the heart of God, which can help us work through our feelings about our story.

Choose a scripture (below) that reinforces God's Truth about your feelings of anger and frustration. Then use that scripture to do a spiritual formation experience explained below.

Be quick to listen, but slow to speak. And be slow to become angry, for human anger is never a legitimate tool to promote God's righteous purpose. (James 1:19-20, TPT)

A gentle answer makes anger disappear, but a rough answer makes it grow. (Prov. 15:1, ERV)

When you are angry, don't let it carry you into sin. Don't let the sun set with anger in your heart or give the devil room to work. (Eph. 4:26-27, Voice)

The Lord is compassionate and merciful, slow to get angry and filled with unfailing love. (Psa. 103:8, NLT)

Think long; think hard. When you are angry, don't let it carry you into sin. When night comes, in calm be silent. (Psa. 4:4, Voice)

Spiritual Formation Experience

Recall a place from your personal history that felt safe. Imagine God being there with you.

Meditate on the verse of scripture that you chose above, saying it softly, over & over to yourself until you can say it or a portion of it with your eyes closed. (As you repeat this scripture, allow yourself to see it with the eyes of your heart.)

Journal your response to these questions:

1. What is the picture you see in your mind's eye as you repeat the scripture?

_____

_____

_____

_____

2. What does the scripture reveal about the heart of God?

_____

_____

_____

_____

3. Put yourself in the picture of this scripture. What is the Lord speaking to you personally in this scripture?

_____

_____

_____

_____

4. Take time to pray, saying to God what you have seen and heard from Him today through this experience.

Finding Purpose in Your Story: Reframing its Meaning

Think back on the story you wrote about feeling angry or controlled. Here are some questions to help you in finding a purpose for your story:

What has God taught you, and how have you grown as a result of this story?

_____

_____

_____

_____

What are some good things that have come from it (blessings, coincidences, miracles, healing, etc.)?

_____

_____

_____

_____

Color and Share

Studies show that coloring can help you slow down your heart rate, giving you a sense of calm. Try concentrating only on coloring in a non-competitive way, and you will experience a change in your feelings and mood. To print additional journal or coloring pages, go to GwenEbner.com/free.

While you color on the page I have provided, share with God (in prayer) or with someone else how you have found purpose in your story. *(Feel free to use your answers from the questions above.)*

If you are sharing your thoughts with God, you can do it out loud or write it on the lines below:

_____

_____

_____

_____

_____

_____

_____

_____

_____

> *Check out the extra information in Appendix D if you want to go deeper in this healing process.*

In Christ
I am Free

CHAPTER 6

❧

The Need to Be Perfect

When I turned eight, I began taking piano lessons. At first, it was fun, but then Mom started to make me practice every day. I wanted to quit taking piano lessons, but my parents said I couldn't. Instead, they offered me rewards if I practiced, and consequences if I didn't. She said she would do the dishes at suppertime if I practiced the piano at the same time. It was a deal!

After taking lessons for a while, the teacher said I would be playing in a recital. I felt butterflies when I performed for the first time in front of a crowd. It helped that the teacher allowed me to use my book as I played. However, after that recital, she said I would need to play the next one by memory.

When that recital day came, my stomach churned as I waited to play. Finally, it was my turn, and I sat down and began to play the first section of the song. But when I got to the second section, my mind went blank. So, I went back and started from the beginning again. However, when I got to the second section again, I still couldn't remember the notes to play.

My cheeks turned red, and my heart began to pound as I quickly got up from the piano and hurried back to my seat. I sat down and slumped in my chair as I felt the tears roll down my face. I felt like a failure and began to dread going home.

I had learned from experience that Dad would criticize me for my mistakes. Sure enough, my father had words for me when we arrived home, which left my heart in turmoil. I felt hurt but also angry with myself for messing up at something I had practiced for hours. Why was I never able to please my dad?

When I was nine years old, Dad offered me a reward of $10.00 if I got all A's on my report card. That would be equal to $100.00 today, a lot of money for a 9-year-old. I was full of excitement because that was something I could do! But the catch was that if I didn't get all A's, I only got $1.00 for each A.

The day came when the teacher sent our report cards home with us. My throat was dry as I handed the grade card to my dad. I had gotten 3 A's and 1 B+. I saw the look on my father's face. I'm not sure whether I was more upset at disappointing Dad or at getting only $3 instead of $10. Why couldn't I be perfect?

At age ten, my family moved from our house on Lynn Drive to a big two-story yellow brick home on Central Avenue, within walking distance to our school. This home had a big kitchen with a large table, located in an area surrounded by windows. We spent a lot of time in the kitchen as a family - eating, talking, and playing games. One day Mom announced that Donna and I were responsible for doing the dishes after each meal and we were to take turns washing and drying them.

On one particular day, it was Donna's turn to wash and my turn to dry and put the dishes in the cabinet. We were laughing and saying silly things, just like girls our age often did. As we neared the end of our task, Dad arrived home from work. As he came over to the cabinet, I noticed the stern, tired look on his face. I started getting a knot in my stomach because I knew what that meant.

As Dad reached into the cabinet and took hold of a glass, I saw a frown began to form on his face. He told me that the glass was still wet. Immediately the look in his eyes changed, and his voice became irritated, "Gwen, why aren't the dishes completely dried?" And before I knew it, he was angrily pulling one glass after another out of the cabinet and throwing them back into the water to be washed and dried again, correctly!

I found myself shaking inside as I realized Dad's anger was aimed at me. Once again, I had not measured up to his expectations.

I made an inner vow that day: I would not let Dad hurt me ever again. I would close my heart so that would never happen again.

~ From this experience, I had _feelings_ of rejection and not feeling good enough.
~ The _lie_ I believed was that I had to be perfect to be loved.
~ The way I _coped_ with these feelings was to try harder, so I could be perfect.

Finding Purpose in My Story: Reframing its Meaning

Music was important in our family, especially to dad. As a child, he heard a man on the street playing the harmonica. He was curious and stopped to talk to him. The man said he'd give Dad the harmonica if he'd learn to play it. Dad got the man's harmonica and learned on his own to play. As an adult, he played in church and other places.

Even though I felt criticized many times by Dad, things began to look up when he surprised me with a request. He asked Donna and me to teach him how to sing tenor. We agreed and spent many hours practicing with Dad and eventually formed a trio. I sang soprano, Donna sang alto, and Dad sang tenor. We enjoyed many years singing together in church.

As an adult, he and I enjoyed playing harmonica and piano duets in church. Weekly, I played the organ in church and participated in school musical events. I ended up majoring in music education and music therapy in college. I enjoyed many years of musical experiences.

Because of wanting to be perfect, I drove myself to finish an undergraduate degree in music education and a master's degree in counseling. One day while I was working on my Ph.D. in Marriage and Family Services, I said to myself, "Gwen, your dad doesn't even have a high school diploma. Why are you trying so hard to get a Ph.D.? Is it so that you can prove to your dad that you are worthwhile?" I felt God say that I didn't need to do that because I was good enough. Period! And that I would never need to prove my worth because Jesus had done that at the cross when he died for me!

I did finish my Ph.D. and spent fifteen years as a professor at Winebrenner Seminary. Teaching and challenging students turned out to be one of my greatest passions, and one I will never regret. Even though I did not have the right motive for getting that degree, God used me in that position to help many students going into ministry.

In 2002 a challenging marital issue motivated me to begin the process of inner healing. I ended up going to several workshops, including *The Healing of the Inner Child* and *The Process of Inner Healing*.

One day in 2004 I went to see Dad and share my feelings about my childhood hurts. I showed him a picture of he and I holding hands when I was five years old. I went on to tell him that I felt like he had dropped my hand after the car accident.

He and I had a healing conversation that day about some of my childhood hurts. He put his arms around me and told me that he was sorry and that he had always thought I was terrific. He had only wanted me to have a better chance in life than he had as an orphan.

Since my dad lived near me, I got to spend eight more years building a relationship with him. Thankfully, that happened because God allowed him to live until the age of 96.

One day I sensed God encouraging me to change the

way I spoke about the criticism I had received from Dad. Instead of saying Dad 'criticized' me a lot, I could say he 'corrected' me sometimes. Even this simple changing of words made a difference in how I felt about my dad.

Your Story

Recall a story (preferably in your childhood) when you felt rejected and not good enough. In the lines below, write where you were, your age and the situation that took place.

_____

_____

_____

_____

_____

_____

_____

_____

_____

_____

_____

_____

_____

_____

_____

Connecting with God

We will use a scriptural process to experience the heart of God, which can help us work through our feelings about our story.

Choose a scripture (below) that reinforces God's Truth about the issue of rejection. Then use that scripture to do a spiritual formation experience explained below.

For the Holy Spirit makes God's fatherhood real to us as he whispers into our innermost being, 'You are God's beloved child!' (Rom. 8:16, TPT)

I have loved you with an everlasting love. With unfailing love, I have drawn you to myself (Jer. 31:3, NLT)

Can a mother forget the baby at her breast and have no compassion on the child she has borne? Though she may forget, I will not forget you! See, I have engraved you on the palms of my hands; your walls are ever before me. (Isa. 49:15-16, NIV)

Even if my father and mother abandon me, the Lord will hold me close. (Psa. 27:10, NLT)

And I am convinced that nothing can ever separate us from God's love. (Rom. 8:38, NLT)

Spiritual Formation Experience

Recall a place from your personal history that felt safe. Imagine God being there with you.

Meditate on the verse of scripture that you chose above, saying it softly, over & over to yourself until you can say it or a portion of it with your eyes closed. (As you repeat this scripture, allow yourself to see it with the eyes of your heart.)

Journal your response to these questions:

1. What is the picture you see in your mind's eye as you repeat the scripture?

_____

_____

_____

_____

2. What does the scripture reveal about the heart of God?

_____

_____

_____

_____

3. Put yourself in the picture of this scripture. What is the Lord speaking to you personally in this scripture?

_____

_____

_____

_____

4. Take time to pray, saying to God what you have seen and heard from Him today through this experience.

Finding Purpose in Your Story: Reframing its Meaning

Think back on the story you wrote about feeling rejected and not good enough. Here are some questions to help you in finding a purpose for your story:

What has God taught you, and how have you grown as a result of this story?

_____

_____

_____

_____

What are some good things that have come from it (blessings, coincidences, miracles, healing, etc.)?

_____

_____

_____

_____

Color and Share

Studies show that coloring can help you slow down your heart rate, giving you a sense of calm. Try concentrating only on coloring in a non-competitive way, and you will experience a change in your feelings and mood. To print additional journal or coloring pages, go to GwenEbner.com/free.

While you color on the page I have provided, share with God (in prayer) or with someone else how you have found purpose in your story. *(Feel free to use your answers from the questions above.)*

If you are sharing your thoughts with God, you can do it out loud or write it on the lines below:

_____

_____

_____

_____

_____

_____

_____

_____

Check out the extra information in Appendix D if you want to go deeper in this healing process.

You are

Worthy of Love

This is your final assignment:

I encourage you to pay attention
to times in your life when you
are <u>triggered</u> by one of the
feelings in these six chapters:
insecurity, shame, fear, anxiety,
anger or rejection.
Then, go back to the situation
in which you first experienced
this feeling and invite
God into that situation.
Ask him to heal you of the hurt
that took place that day.
Then thank him for his healing touch!

God bless you as you
allow God to heal your heart,
just as he has mine!

Jesus endured the punishment that made us completely
whole, and in his wounding, we found our healing.
(Isaiah 53:5, TPT)

May you always remember that Jesus suffered
and died so that you can be healed!

Feeling Profiles

Feeling Profile 1 (from hurts)

Put a number beside the words below that you feel (or have felt) most often.

0 – Never   1 – Sometimes   2 – Regularly

Then add up a total for each column.

(These coincide with each chapter & will help you determine which ones you feel most often).

Insecure *(Ch. 1)*
___ Unsafe
___ Unconfident
___ Helpless
___ Powerless
___ Vulnerable

___ TOTAL
Feeling: I am not safe

Ashamed *(Ch. 2)*
___ Embarrassed
___ Violated
___ Guarded heart
___ Self-Conscious
___ Humiliated

___ TOTAL
Feeling: It's my fault

Afraid *(Ch. 3)*
___ Nervous
___ Frightened
___ Scared
___ Terrified
___ Panicky

___ TOTAL
Feeling: I am alone

Anxious *(Ch. 4)*
___ Uncomfortable
___ Uneasy
___ Distressed
___ Uptight
___ Edgy

___ TOTAL
Feeling: I feel agitated

Angry (Ch. 5)
___ Mad
___ Irritated
___ Annoyed
___ Frustrated
___ Bothered

___ TOTAL
Feeling: I hate being controlled

Rejected (Ch. 6)
___ Abandoned
___ Unwanted
___ Excluded
___ Ignored
___ Criticized

___ TOTAL
Feeling: Not worthwhile

Feeling Profile 2

God can help us replace our negative feelings with positives ones. Put a number beside the words below that you are starting to feel more often.

0 – Never   1 – Sometimes   2 – Regularly

Then add up a total for each column.

Which of the following are you growing in the most?

Secure *(Ch. 1)*
___ Safe
___ Confident
___ Secure
___ Protected
___ God is holding me

___ TOTAL

Confident *(Ch. 2)*
___ Open heart
___ Respected
___ Comfortable with self
___ Self-Confident
___ Approved

___ TOTAL

Fearless *(Ch. 3)*
___ Courageous
___ Faith
___ Unafraid
___ Assurance
___ Boldness

___ TOTAL

Peaceful *(Ch. 4)*
___ Tranquility
___ Calm
___ Relaxed
___ Soothed
___ Serene

___ TOTAL

Assertive *(Ch. 5)*
___ Self-controlled
___ Untroubled
___ Decisive
___ Unprovoked
___ Contained

___ TOTAL

Cherished *(Ch. 6)*
___ Feel cared for
___ Wanted
___ Included
___ Noticed
___ Affirmed

___ TOTAL

❦

Scriptural Affirmations

Each chapter lists a feeling I experienced.
Use these affirmations, based on scripture, to help reinforce
what God wants you to believe.

Safe & Secure, instead of Insecure & Unsafe (Chapter 1)
- God's everlasting arms are under me (Deut. 33:27)
- God is a safe place for me to hide (Psa. 46:1)
- God's wrap-around presence surrounds me (Psa. 125:2)
- God's strong right hand holds me securely (Psa. 63:7-8)
- When I run to God, I am safe (Prov. 18:10)
- God protects me as the apple of his eye (Deut. 32:10)
- God's outstretched arms protect me and under them I am perfectly safe (Psa. 91:4)

Confident in Christ, instead of Ashamed (Chapter 2)
- I am complete in Christ (Col. 2:9-10)
- God is restoring me and making me strong, firm and steadfast (I Pet. 5:10)
- I am an incredible work of art; God's masterpiece. (Ep. 2:10)

- God will restore and heal my wounds (Jer. 30:17)
- God's steadfast love never ceases; his mercies never come to an end (Lam. 3:22-23)

Faith in Christ, instead of Fear (Chapter 3)
- I will not fear because God is with me (Isa. 41:10)
- When I seek the Lord, he delivers me from all of my fears (Psa. 34:4)
- I will put my trust and faith in God when I am afraid (Psa. 56:3)
- I am not afraid because God promises to help me (Isa. 41:13)
- I will not be afraid because God's perfect love takes away my fear (I Jn. 4:18)
- God calms my fears with his love. (Zeph. 3:17)
- God will be with me, each and every day. (Matt. 28:20)

Calm and Content, instead of Anxious (Chapter 4)
- I am loved by God with an everlasting love (Jer. 31:3)
- I can rely on God's faithful love (Isa. 54:10)
- God takes delight in me and rejoices over me with song (Zeph. 3:17)
- I am worth more than a flock of sparrows (Matt. 10:31)
- I am cherished by God and every moment he is thinking of me (Psa. 139:17)
- God has written my name on the palm of his hands (Isa. 49:15-16)
- God notices me and even knows the number of hairs on my head (Matt. 10:31)

- I am precious to God and he loves me (Isa. 43:4)
- Jesus loves me and proved it by giving his own life for me (Jn. 3:16)
- I am the apple of God's eye. (Deut. 32:10)
- God's loyal love for me will never run out; his mercies are new every morning. (Lam. 3:22-23)
- The mountains may move and the hills disappear, but even then God's faithful love for me will not be shaken. (Isa. 54:10)
- God will hold me in his arms, now and forever. (Psa. 125:2)

Free in Christ, instead of angry (Chapter 5)
- I choose to be quick to listen, slow to speak and slow to become angry. (James 1:19-20)
- I choose to reply with a gentle response, instead of a harsh answer. (Prov. 15:1)
- I will not carry my anger into the next day and give the devil a foothold in my life. (Eph. 4:26-27)
- I want to become like the Lord, compassionate, merciful and slow to get angry. (Psa. 103:8)
- I will meditate and be still when I am angry. (Psa. 4:4)

Cherished in Christ, instead of Rejected (Chapter 6)
- God whispers into my innermost being these words, 'You are God's beloved child'. (Rom. 8:16)
- God draws me close as he tells me that he loves me with an everlasting love. (Jer. 31:3)
- God will never forget me. He has written my name on the palms of his hands (Isa. 49:15-16)

- Even if my father and mother abandon me, God will hold me close. (Psa. 27:10)
- I am convinced that nothing can ever separate me from God's love. (Rom. 8:38)
- God will never abandon me. (Psa. 16:10, Deut. 4:31)

❦

Exchanging Lies for Truth
(A summary of the process)

- "Lord, I confess the sin of believing the lie that
  _____. I ask you GOD to forgive me
  for believing this lie.
- I also forgive MYSELF for believing this lie and living
  my life according to it.
- I break the power of this lie and exchange it for God's
  truth that says, _____

_____

Ch. 1 – *I feel Insecure*	**Ch. 2 – *I feel Ashamed***
LIE: I am not Safe	**LIE:** It is my fault
God's Truth:	**God's Truth:**
I am safe in Christ	I am good enough
Scriptures:	**Scriptures:**
Deut. 33:27 (NLT)	Col. 2:9-10 (NLT)
Psa. 46:1 (MSG)	I Peter 5:10 (NIV)
Prov. 18:10 (NLT)	Eph. 2:10 (NLT)
Psa. 125:2 (TPT)	Jer. 30:17 (NIV)
Psa. 63:7-8 (NLT)	Lam. 3:22-23 (ISV)

Ch. 3 – *I feel Afraid*
LIE: I am alone

God's Truth:
God is with me

Scriptures:
Isa. 41:10 (NIV)
Psa. 34:4 (NIV)
Psa. 56:3 (NIV)
Isa. 41:13 (NIV)
I Jn. 4:18 (ERV)

Ch. 4 – *I feel Anxious*
LIE: I am powerless

God's Truth:
God gives me peace

Scriptures:
Phil. 4:6-7 (NIV)
I Peter 5:7 (NIV)
Psa. 94:19 (ISV)
Isa. 35:4 (ISV)
Isa. 41:10 (ISV)

Ch. 5 – *I feel Angry*
Lie: People control me

God's Truth:
God is in control

Scriptures:
James 1:19-20 (TPT)
Prov. 15:1 (ERV)
Eph. 4:26-27 (Voice)
Psa. 103:8 (NLT)
Psa. 4:4 (Voice)

Ch. 6 - *I feel Rejected*
Lie: I'm not worthy of love

God's Truth:
God accepts me

Scriptures:
Romans 8:16 (TPT)
Jer. 31:3 (NLT)
Isa. 49:15-16 (NIV)
Psa. 27:10 (NLT)
Romans 8:38 (NLT)

Going Deeper

Chapter 1

After each story, I reflected on three things: the feelings I experienced, the lie I accepted, and the coping skills I used. Now it's your turn to do this.

1. Reread the story you wrote in chapter one about feeling insecure or unsafe.

2. Identify a lie you believed when you felt insecure or unsafe.

   _____

   _____

   _____

3. What are some healthy or unhealthy ways you coped with these feelings?

   _____

   _____

   _____

   _____

The Exchange

Here is a process for exchanging lies with God's Truth. Here's my example:

- Lord, I confess the sin of believing the lie that "I am not safe anywhere." I ask you to forgive me for believing this lie."
- I forgive myself for believing this lie and living my life according to it.
- I break the power of this lie and exchange it for the Truth of God that says, "I am safe and secure in God's arms."

It's Your Turn

Now use these same steps to exchange the lie that came to your mind as you journaled in chapter one.

- I confess to you, Lord, the sin of believing the lie _____. I ask you to forgive me for believing this lie.
- I forgive _myself_ for believing this lie and living my life according to it.
- I break the power of this lie and exchange it for the Truth of God that says, _____

_____

_____.

Chapter 2

After each story, I reflected on three things: the feelings I experienced, the lie I accepted, and the coping skills I used. Now it's your turn to do this.

1. Reread the story you wrote in chapter two about feeling ashamed.

2. Identify a lie you believed when you felt that shame

   _____

   _____

   _____

   _____

3. What are some healthy or unhealthy ways you coped with these feelings?

   _____

   _____

   _____

   _____

The Exchange

Here is a process for exchanging lies with God's Truth.
Here's my example:

- Lord, I confess the sin of believing the lie that
  "<u>Because I did something wrong, I'm not okay.</u>" I ask
  you to forgive me for believing this lie."
- I forgive myself for believing this lie and living my
  life according to it.
- I break the power of this lie and exchange it for the
  Truth of God that says, "<u>Jesus is not ashamed of me.
  He loves and forgives me.</u>"

It's Your Turn

Now use these same steps to exchange the lie that came
to your mind as you journaled in chapter two.

- I confess to you, Lord, the sin of believing the lie
  _____. I ask you to forgive me for
  believing this lie.
- I forgive myself for believing this lie and living my
  life according to it.
- I break the power of this lie and exchange it for the
  Truth of God that says, _____
  _____
  _____.

Chapter 3

After each story, I reflected on three things: the feelings I experienced, the lie I accepted, and the coping skills I used. Now it's your turn to do this.

1. Reread the story you wrote in chapter three about feeling afraid.

2. Identify a lie you believed when you felt afraid

   _____

   _____

   _____

   _____

3. What are some healthy or unhealthy ways you cope with this feeling?

   _____

   _____

   _____

   _____

The Exchange

Here is a process for exchanging lies with God's Truth. Here's my example:

- Lord, I confess the sin of believing the lie that "<u>I am afraid and alone."</u> I ask you to forgive me for believing this lie."
- I forgive myself for believing this lie and living my life according to it.
- I break the power of this lie and exchange it for the Truth of God that says, "<u>God's perfect love takes away fear.</u>"

It's Your Turn

Now I use these same steps to exchange the lie that came to your mind as you journaled in chapter three.

- I confess to you, Lord, the sin of believing the lie _____. I ask you to forgive me for believing this lie.
- I forgive *myself* for believing this lie and living my life according to it.
- I break the power of this lie and exchange it for the Truth of God that says, _____.

Chapter 4

After each story, I reflected on three things: the feelings I experienced, the lie I accepted, and the coping skills I used. Now it's your turn to do this.

1. Reread the story you wrote in chapter four about feeling anxious and uneasy

2. Identify a lie you believed when you felt anxious and uneasy.

   _____

   _____

   _____

   _____

3. What are some healthy or unhealthy ways you cope with these feelings?

   _____

   _____

   _____

   _____

The Exchange

Here is a process for exchanging lies with God's Truth. Here's my example:

- Lord, I confess the sin of believing the lie that "<u>I need to be in control of situations that make me anxious.</u>" I ask you to forgive me for believing this lie."
- I forgive myself for believing this lie and living my life according to it.
- I break the power of this lie and exchange it for the Truth of God that says, "<u>I can cast all my anxiety on the Lord because he cares for me.</u>"

It's Your Turn

Now use these same steps to exchange the lie that came to your mind as you journaled in chapter four.

- I confess to you, Lord, the sin of believing the lie _____. I ask you to forgive me for believing this lie.
- I forgive *myself* for believing this lie and living my life according to it.
- I break the power of this lie and exchange it for the Truth of God that says, _____
  _____
  _____.

Chapter 5

After each story, I reflected on three things: the feelings I experienced, the lie I accepted, and the coping skills I used. Now it's your turn to do this.

1. Reread the story you wrote in chapter five about feeling angry or allowing someone else to control you.

2. Identify a lie you believed when you felt like that.

   _____

   _____

   _____

   _____

3. What are some healthy or unhealthy ways you coped with these feelings?

   _____

   _____

   _____

   _____

The Exchange

Here is a process for exchanging lies with God's Truth.
Here's my example:

- Lord, I confess the sin of believing the lie that "<u>I must allow other people to control me.</u>" I ask you to forgive me for believing this lie."
- I forgive myself for believing this lie and living my life according to it.
- I break the power of this lie and exchange it for the Truth of God that says, "<u>I am not in control, but am deeply loved by the one who is</u>.

It's Your Turn

Now I use these same steps to exchange the lie that came to your mind as you journaled in chapter five.

- I confess to you, Lord, the sin of believing the lie _____. I ask you to forgive me for believing this lie.
- I forgive myself for believing this lie and living my life according to it.
- I break the power of this lie and exchange it for the Truth of God that says, _____ _____ _____.

Chapter 6

After each story, I reflected on three things: the feelings I experienced, the lie I accepted, and the coping skills I used. Now it's your turn to do this.

1. Reread the story you wrote in chapter six about feeling rejected and not good enough.

2. Identify a lie you believed when you felt rejected and not good enough

   _____

   _____

   _____

   _____

3. What are some healthy or unhealthy ways you coped with these feelings?

   _____

   _____

   _____

   _____

The Exchange

Here is a process for exchanging lies with God's Truth. Here's my example:

- Lord, I confess the sin of believing the lie that "I am rejected and not good enough." I ask you to forgive me for believing this lie."
- I forgive myself for believing this lie and living my life according to it.
- I break the power of this lie and exchange it for the Truth of God that says, "I am good enough because I am complete in Christ."

It's Your Turn

Now I use these same steps to exchange the lie that came to your mind as you journaled in chapter 1.

- I confess to you, Lord, the sin of believing the lie _____. I ask you to forgive me for believing this lie.
- I forgive *myself* for believing this lie and living my life according to it.
- I break the power of this lie and exchange it for the Truth of God that says, _____
  _____
  _____.

Group Leader's Guide

This book can be used as a 6-week group study, as well as an individual experience. Each group will be unique, so I pray that you will allow the Holy Spirit to guide you in what you should do.

This study may bring up feelings in those who attend your group as they remember their own stories.

Here are some ways to be prepared:

- Pray each week (by name) for the people who are attending your group
- Try to build connection and trust during the first session, so they feel free to share what they are feeling. You might even consider having them choose someone in the group to be their prayer partner during the study.
- Remind the participants that "what's shared in the group, stays in the group."
- Gather some names of local counselors or pastors that may be available if they need someone to talk to (see Appendix F for online suggestions)
- Consider having some suggestions for resources, books, videos, websites, etc., for the participants (see Appendix F for a few ideas)

- Suggest that they complete the profile in Appendix A, which will help them be aware of some of their strongest feelings. These are the emotions I felt after my story, as noted in each chapter. They will have a chance to work on that feeling themselves as they go through each chapter.
- Have crayons or coloring pencils available for the time when they do the coloring page. Or you can have them bring their own.

Studies show that coloring can help us slow our heart rate down, giving us a sense of calm. What our brain needs is pattern, repetition, and control; coloring can provide that. When a person concentrates only on coloring in a non-competitive way, it can positively affect their feelings and mood.

APPENDIX F

❧

Recommended Resources

Broken Crayons Still Color: From our Mess to God's Masterpiece by Shelley Hitz (Body and Soul Publishing, 2016)

EFT (Emotional Freedom Techniques) for Christians by Sherrie Rice Smith (Energy Psychology Press, 2015)

Healing the Wounded Heart by Thom Gardner (Destiny Image Publishers, 2005)

Illuminate Prayer Journal by CJ & Shelley Hitz (Body and Soul Publishing, 2019)

Intimate Moments with the Father by Gwen Ebner (Path to Wholeness Publishing, 2013)

Jesus Today: Experiencing Hope Through His Presence by Sarah Young (Thomas Nelson, Inc, 2012)

Peace in Anxious Times by Gwen Ebner and Stacey Reeder (Path to Wholeness Publishing, 2016)

The Healing Journey: An Interactive Guide to Spiritual Wholeness by Thom Gardner (Destiny Image Publishers, 2010)

The Tapping Solution: A Revolutionary System for Stress-Free Living by Nick Ortner (Hay House, 2014) Also, he has a book called, The Tapping Solution for Pain Relief (Hay House, 2015)

Gwen Ebner's Website, "Path to Wholeness"

www.gwenebner.com

To print additional coloring pages, go to
GwenEbner.com/free.

Finding a Counselor

- **American Association of Christian Counselors (https://www.aacc.net/)** Click on 'Find a Counselor'
- **Focus on the Family (https://www.focusonthefamily.com/)** Click on 'Get Help'
- **Psychology Today (https://www.psychologytoday.com/us)** Click on 'Get Help'
- To find a Christian who does **counseling online,** google the words "online Christian counselors"